Cooperative Learning

by
Eileen Veronica Hilke

Library of Congress Catalog Card Number 90-60220
ISBN 0-87367-299-2
Copyright © 1990 by the Phi Delta Kappa Educational Foundation
Bloomington, Indiana

This fastback is sponsored by the Decatur Illinois Chapter of Phi Delta Kappa, which made a generous contribution toward publication costs.

The chapter sponsors this fastback to honor Ruth Cortright, past president of the chapter, for her steady and strong leadership, which has contributed to the effectiveness of our chapter, our schools, and our community.

Table of Contents

Introduction

Cooperative learning is more than a catch-phrase for educators. It embodies specific strategies designed to help students work together in groups in order to accomplish both cognitive and affective goals.

In contrast to most school learning in which individuals compete with each other, cooperative learning is an instructional strategy wherein students in small heterogeneous groups share responsibility for learning. As a result, students learn from one another. They learn to appreciate each other's differences and build on individual strengths in order to meet group goals. They learn social skills as well as subject matter.

Several researchers have found that cooperative learning strategies boost individual self-esteem and encourage students to take control of their own learning. This fastback provides an overview of cooperative learning strategies and shows how teachers can integrate these strategies into their instructional plans.

Definition of Cooperative Learning

Cooperative learning is an organizational structure in which a group of students pursue academic goals through collaborative efforts. Students work together in small groups, draw on each other's strengths, and assist each other in completing a task. This method encourages supportive relationships, good communication skills, and higher-level thinking abilities.

The goals of cooperative learning are: 1) to foster academic cooperation among students, 2) to encourage positive group relationships, 3) to develop students' self-esteem, and 4) to enhance academic achievement.

Students can pursue instructional goals in three ways: competitively, individually, or cooperatively. In the 1940s Morton Deutsch (1949) formalized a theory about how people relate and interact in each of these settings. In a competitive setting, students work against each other and their performance is compared. Some students experience failure in this setting, resulting in loss of self-esteem and sometimes in negative feelings toward their higher-achieving peers. In an individualized setting, students work independently at their own pace to attain the goals established by the teacher. The teacher then evaluates the goals set for each individual.

In a cooperative setting, heterogeneous groups of students work together to meet a goal. Each person is responsible for his own learning *and* for assisting others. The strengths of each person are utilized, and success is attainable for every person in the group. Good communication and social skills are needed in order to develop a good working relationship. "Within cooperative learning groups, there tends to be considerable peer regulation, feedback, support and encouragement of learning. Such peer academic support is unavailable in competitive and individualistic learning situations" (Johnson and Johnson 1987).

Basic Elements in Cooperative Learning

Johnson and Johnson (1989) identify five basic elements in cooperative learning: 1) positive goal interdependence, 2) face-to-face promotive interaction, 3) individual accountability, 4) social skills, and 5) group processing. A discussion of each of these elements follows.

Positive Goal Interdependence. Positive goal interdependence occurs when students undertake a group task with a feeling of mutuality. They feel a need to do their own part for the benefit of the entire group. For example, if the group task is to research and write a report, the grade for the report is a group grade. The low achievers in the group strive to do their best for the welfare of the entire group. The high achievers, wanting to maintain their own high quality of work, will assist others in accomplishing the group task. Thus each individual gains a sense of importance and self-worth. Johnson and Johnson et al. (1984) contend that positive interdependence is achieved:

> through mutual goals (goal interdependence); divisions of labor (task interdependence); dividing materials, resources, or information among group members (resource interdependence); assigning students differing roles (role interdependence); and by giving joint rewards (reward interdependence). In order for a learning situation to be cooperative, students must perceive that they are positively interdependent with other members of their learning group.

10

Face-to-Face Promotive Interaction. Promotive interaction occurs when a verbal interchange takes place where students explain how they obtained an answer or how a problem might be solved. They can also help each other understand a task. Students check each other's comprehension and ask questions of group members before asking the teacher for clarification. When a task is completed, group members summarize what was learned.

Individual Accountability. Individual accountability is taking personal responsibility for learning material. In addition to contributing to the group, each student needs to master certain material. Once the teacher determines the level of mastery, then group members offer support and assist each other in attaining the mastery level.

A question that often comes up in discussions about cooperative learning is what to do about the student who does not participate, allows others to do the work, and fails to learn the basic content. To prevent this from happening, a teacher can average individual exam scores for a group grade. Thus when one low exam score lowers the average, peers will exert not too subtle pressure on the individual to study harder. Or they will see the need to work with the individual in order to achieve mastery level. Also from time to time, the teacher may select individual assignments to grade, which encourages all group members to complete their work in a timely and acceptable manner.

Social Skills. Critical to the success of cooperative learning are such social skills as knowing how to communicate effectively and how to develop respect and trust within the group. Well-functioning groups do not just happen; students need guidance in how to follow as well as to lead. When responsibility for learning is shared, students need to encourage each other to complete the assigned task. They need to know how to ask for assistance when they need it. When conflict arises (and it will), students need to know how to use conflict resolution strategies.

Group Processing. Periodically students need to reflect on how well the group is working and to analyze how their effectiveness might be improved. This is called group processing. Observations by group members, the teacher, or an individual assigned the role of observer can provide the feedback that is essential for group processing. An observer might record what happened in the group when planning a project about which there were strong differences of opinion. With this feedback, the students can move on to finding a solution and to offering suggestions for handling such disputes in the future. Out of this process, the group might conclude: "We have made a good beginning in planning the project, but we need to work harder at listening to everyone's ideas."

Structuring Cooperative Learning

For cooperative learning to be successful, the teacher must carefully plan the group experience, monitor the group process during the experience, and then evaluate the experience. Each of these steps is discussed below.

Prior to assigning students to work in groups, the teacher needs to identify a task or project for the group and decide how to teach the task objectives. This requires a clear explanation of the task to be completed and explicit directions for the procedures to be followed. The teacher might need to define key terminology and concepts and relate them to previous learning. This will aid in comprehension and retention when the group begins to work on its own.

The next step is to assign students to groups. Groups will vary in size depending on the task and experience of the students. In general, groups should be kept small — three to five students. They should be heterogeneous in terms of academic ability, with attention also to gender and racial mix. Desks or tables should then be arranged so students in a group sit together and face each other.

Just placing students in groups does not ensure cooperative learning. They must be taught the social skills essential for effective group functioning. These include seeing that everyone participates, listening carefully and critically, taking turns, assisting those who have difficulty understanding, explaining the reasons for one's answer, and respecting each other's viewpoints.

Having students develop their own list of behavior skills will give them a sense of ownership of the group processes. Also, students must have many opportunities to practice the skills. This will require setting up situations in which the skills can be used and reinforced until they become incorporated into the students' behavioral repertoires.

In monitoring the group, the teacher must make sure everyone is participating. One way of doing this is to assign roles to each group member; for example, recorder, resource person, and summarizer. By walking around the room, the teacher can monitor how well each group is doing with both the academic content and the group process. As the group members learn to rely on each other and become a well-functioning unit, the teacher will find less need to intervene.

Problems sometimes arise in cooperative learning groups. Some typical problems are the student who tries to do all the work alone, the student who dominates the decision making for the entire group, or the student who won't participate. These problems can be solved by assigning roles for each group member and evaluating the group's progress by how well each student performs the assigned role. For students who are reluctant to participate, assigning them a role makes them feel that they are a part of the group and that their contributions are important for the total group performance. Another technique for encouraging group involvement is to "jigsaw" parts of a lesson so that each person has an important piece of information the others don't have. This information is later shared or taught to the rest of the group. This technique stresses the importance of each group member's sharing information in order to complete the task.

When the group task has been completed, time should be provided for an analysis of how well the task was done and how effectively the group functioned. This can be done in a general class discussion or by using evaluation forms like those on page 15.

Personal Evaluation Form

I participated in each activity.	Always	Occasionally	Never
I critically listened to others.	Always	Occasionally	Never
I respected viewpoints of others.	Always	Occasionally	Never
I came prepared to class.	Always	Occasionally	Never
I studied for exams.	Always	Occasionally	Never
I helped others when needed.	Always	Occasionally	Never
I was open-minded.	Always	Occasionally	Never
I took my turn and didn't dominate the discussion.	Always	Occasionally	Never

Group Evaluation Form

We understood the task objectives and procedures.	Always	Occasionally	Never
We assigned tasks to group members.	Always	Occasionally	Never
We practiced cooperative skills.	Always	Occasionally	Never
We reflected on group behaviors.	Always	Occasionally	Never
We discussed group process.	Always	Occasionally	Never
We checked each other's comprehension.	Always	Occasionally	Never
We had confidence in our ability to complete the task.	Always	Occasionally	Never

Variations on the Basic Elements of Cooperative Learning

There are other approaches to cooperative learning that are variations of the basic elements discussed earlier. These include Learning Together/Circles of Learning, Jigsaw, Groups of Four, Co-Op Co-Op, Group Investigation/Small-Group Teaching, Student Team Learning, Cooperative Integrated Reading and Composition, and Team Assisted Individualization. A decision to use one of these variations would depend on the instructor's teaching style and instructional objectives of the group project. Following are brief explanations of each of these approaches.

Learning Together/Circles of Learning

Johnson and Johnson (1975) delineated procedures for implementing cooperative learning using what they called the Learning Together model. The basic idea is to have students work in four- or five-member teams on assignment sheets, with each team handing in a single sheet representing the group effort. The students would receive praise and rewards for their product if done satisfactorily.

In *Circles of Learning* (1984), the Johnsons and their associates refined their techniques. They suggest using heterogeneous groups of two to six students, who share resources and help each other learn. The form of group interaction is decided by the teacher. They suggest 18 steps for structuring cooperative learning, which may be used with any age level or any subject area.

1. Specifying instructional objectives (academic and collaborative skills)
2. Deciding the size of the group
3. Assigning students to groups
4. Arranging the room
5. Planning the instructional materials to promote interdependence
6. Assigning roles to ensure interdependence
7. Explaining the academic task
8. Structuring positive goal interdependence
9. Structuring individual accountability
10. Structuring intergroup cooperation
11. Explaining criteria for success
12. Specifying desired behaviors
13. Monitoring students' behavior
14. Providing task assistance
15. Teaching collaborative skills
16. Providing closure to the lesson
17. Evaluating the quality and quantity of students' learning
18. Assessing how well the group functioned

Jigsaw

Elliot Aronson (1978) developed the Jigsaw cooperative learning model, which uses task specialization. Each student has a task that contributes to an overall group objective. In heterogeneous groups of three to six students, each student is assigned a part of a lesson. Each student works independently to become an expert on a portion of the lesson and is accountable for teaching the information to others in the group as well as mastering the information other group members have provided. The teacher assesses the mastery of the overall topic. Individual grades are given based on an exam.

Groups of Four

Burns (1981) describes the Groups of Four model, which is appropriate for all grade levels and in many curriculum areas. This model does not focus on achieving group goals, nor are individuals in the group accountable for group achievement. Rather, it simply involves having four students work together on some task.

This model is easy to implement. Four randomly selected students sit together and work on a common task. For example, students might review their homework assignment, discuss any differences, decide on the correct answers, and turn in one homework assignment. This encourages discussion and justification of an answer. It also reduces the teacher's time for correcting homework.

The teacher's role includes explaining the group task, presenting the problem, asking for questions, then allowing the groups to work. If the group members are unable to help each other, then the teacher provides assistance. The teacher leads a follow-up discussion. This model reinforces academic attainment and provides practice in social skills.

Co-Op Co-Op

Developed by Kagan (1985), Co-Op Co-Op is designed to provide conditions in which students' natural curiosity, intelligence, and expressiveness will emerge and develop. Co-Op Co-Op is structured around a series of team-building exercises requiring students to interact with each other. First a main topic of study is selected and then subdivided into mini-topics. Each student selects a mini-topic, researches it, and shares the information with the group. After discussion, the information is compiled into a group presentation and given to the entire class. Evaluation covers the student's work in the group, plus individual papers.

Group Investigation/Small-Group Teaching

This model, developed by Sharan and Hertz-Lazarowitz (1980), emphasizes interdependence among groups. The teacher assigns an area of study, and student groups of two to six select a topic related to the area that interests them. Through cooperative planning, the teacher and students decide how to investigate the topic and group tasks are assigned. The teacher helps by setting up workstations around the room where the research is conducted. Each member carries out an individual investigation, then the group summarizes findings and prepares an interesting presentation to share with the entire class. By listening to all of the reports, students gain a broad perspective on the topic; and they are expected to learn all of the material. Evaluation covers both individual and group efforts and is based on observations of how well students use investigative skills. Higher level cognitive skills such as application and synthesis are emphasized.

Student Team Learning

Slavin (1978) describes different methods of cooperative learning that involve competition among teams matched by ability. The emphasis is on achieving team goals, but individual accountability in terms of improving one's own performance is also important. Individual accountability encourages peer tutoring so that each student is prepared for an individual assessment. Even low achievers are challenged to improve their own past performance. Three of the more popular techniques are: Student Team Achievement Divisions (STAD), Teams-Games-Tournaments (TGT), and Jigsaw II, which is Slavin's competitive adaptation of the previously mentioned Jigsaw technique.

Teachers using STAD present new information, then divide the class into heterogeneous groups of four members. The teacher presents a lesson; team members master the information themselves, then assist others in mastering it. Weekly quizzes are given and individual scores recorded. Teachers also record improvement scores when a current quiz score exceeds a past score. Teams that reach a certain criterion level or have a high improvement score receive recognition.

In TGT, student teams earn points for engaging in academic competitions. First, the teacher presents information in a lecture or a lecture-discussion period. Next, students assist each other in studying the teacher-prepared worksheets based on the lecture information. Students then have weekly tournaments where teams of equal ability compete to see who can answer the most questions prepared by the teacher. Points are awarded for a correct answer. Teams with the highest number of points are publicly recognized.

Jigsaw II (Slavin 1986) works most effectively where the goal is learning concepts rather than skills. All students read a common narrative such as a short story. Each student in the four- to five-member group receives an information sheet on a different topic. After reading their sheets, one student from each group meets in a temporary "expert" group composed of students who have studied the same topic. After a discussion period, students return to their original group to teach other group members all they know about their topic. After this process is completed, an individual quiz is given covering all of the topics. Then team certificates are given based on quiz improvement scores.

Cooperative Integrated Reading and Composition (CIRC)

CIRC is a curriculum-specific cooperative learning approach for teaching reading and writing in grades 2-6 (Slavin 1988). The three main components in CIRC are direct instruction in comprehension, basal-related activities, and integrated writing/language arts. The reading component makes use of basal readers and reading groups. But instead of workbook assignments, student team activities are used. For example, the students might help each other to identify the literary elements of plot, characterization, and setting; predict the outcomes of stories; and retell the stories.

The writing/language arts component involves students helping each other in editing original papers or stories. Teaching of language mechanics is integrated with the writing assignments using a language textbook. The cooperative dimension of this model involves two students from different reading groups working as a team. They read to one another, check comprehension, practice spelling, edit writing drafts, and publish books of writing samples. For assessment, students take quizzes when teammates determine they are ready. Students receive reward certificates based on the average performance of all team members.

Team Assisted Individualization (TAI)

TAI, also developed by Slavin (1987), is a mathematics program designed for grades 3-6 that combines cooperative learning with individualized instruction. Most math classes have students with a wide range of skills. The basic premise of this cooperative learning approach is that low achievers can move ahead without holding high-achieving students back. This is accomplished by placing high-, medium-, and low-ability students in teams of four to five members. First, students are pretested and placed in an appropriate point in an individualized program. Students work independently at their own level and do their own assignments. Then students meet in teams, where they exchange papers, check each other's math accuracy, help each other, then take a check-out quiz. At the completion of the unit, students take a final test. Teams receive recognition based on the average number of units completed by team members.

In addition to working with the teams, the teacher's role in TAI is to introduce major concepts using direct instruction prior to students working on their individualized units. At times the teacher does whole group instruction on such skills as measurement and problem solving. The teacher also gives fact tests to the students. Use of this approach has improved students' self-esteem and mathematics achievement.

Selecting a Cooperative Learning Technique

With the variety of cooperative learning techniques available, the teacher must decide which one is most appropriate for the content to be covered and the learning objectives to be achieved. Actually, several techniques might be effective for the same objectives. The list that follows suggests some of the questions a teacher might ask when deciding which technique to use.

1. Do I want competition between the groups? (Teams-Games-Tournament)
2. Do I have an adequate supply and variety of resources for student research? (Group Investigation, Co-Op Co-Op)
3. Do I want to combine cooperative learning with individualized learning in my math class? (Team Assisted Individualization)
4. Do I want to assess student achievement by giving an objective test to the group? (Jigsaw; Student Team Achievement Divisions)
5. Do I feel knowledgeable about a topic so I can give in-depth guidance during student research? (Group Investigation)
6. Do I want to divide the content material into small components? (Jigsaw)
7. Do I want to use a basal reading text but also have some team activities? (Cooperative Integrated Reading and Composition)

Grading Group Work

Traditional grading procedures will require some adaptation for cooperative learning. Prior to starting a cooperative learning task, students should be made aware of how they will be evaluated. By outlining the criteria for successful completion of a task, students will know precisely what is expected of them. The teacher must determine how much weight to give group projects compared to individual assignments and exams. The teacher also might decide to award bonus points if all group members attain a specified criterion level.

A teacher has several options when it is time to assign a letter grade. They include: 1) a group grade for a project completed as a group, 2) average of individual assignment grades with group task grades, 3) randomly select one paper or test to grade and give all group members the grade received on that test, 4) award bonus points or other reward if all students attain the criterion level expected.

Following is an example of how students might be graded in a social studies class studying the culture of another country. In this cooperative learning classroom, each student is expected to complete two group assignments and one individual project and to take a final test. The grades for two students might be as follows:

	Group Project 1	Group Project 2	Individual Project	Final Test	Final Grade
Tom	A –	B +	B +	B	B +
Sue	A –	B +	A	A	A

Another way of grading could be on a point basis, with points earned for group projects, individual project, final test, and extra points if everyone in the group achieves the designated criterion level. The teacher establishes total possible points for each project, final test, and bonus points. A point system of grading might be as follows:

	Group Project 1	Group Project 2	Individual Project	Final Test	Bonus Points	Final Grade
Possible Points	20	20	30	30		100
Tom	18	15	26	25	10	94 = A −
Sue	18	15	30	30	10	103 = A

If the teacher has established that 95-100 points would be an A, 90-94 points an A −, 85-89 a B +, and so on, then Tom's grade would be an A −, while Sue with her 10 bonus points would be an A. When a part of the grade is based on group work, then students soon realize the importance of being a contributing member of the group.

Initially, students (and sometimes their parents) might complain that a single group grade is not fair. However, after students have had experience working in cooperative groups, their opinion changes. They realize they are in control; they can help others and be helped by others in meeting established goals successfully. They come to accept a group grade because everyone provided input into the learning process. By including grades for individual work, final tests, and bonus points for group achievement, most concerns about grading equity can be alleviated.

What Research Says About Cooperative Learning

This chapter summarizes what researchers have found regarding the outcomes of cooperative learning. It covers academic achievement, intergroup relations, provisions for mainstreamed students, and student self-esteem.

Academic Achievement

In general, researchers have found an increase in academic achievement when cooperative learning is used at both the elementary and secondary levels. In addition, research conducted in both urban and rural settings on achievement in social studies, language arts, math, science, and reading found that student achievement increased. Although academic achievement has been positive, more important are the factors or conditions that researchers believe contribute to the positive results. Many studies conclude that group goals and individual accountability are two basic elements in cooperative learning that contribute to student achievement. When students understand that their individual contributions are necessary to achieve the group goal, the motivation to achieve is strong.

In Slavin's (1986) review of 35 studies, he found the effects of cooperative learning on achievement to be overwhelmingly positive:

> Twenty-nine of these (83%) found that students in Student Team Learning classes gained significantly more in achievement than did students in traditionally taught classes studying the same objectives.

None found differences favoring control groups. The methodological quality of the studies is very high; most used random assignment to experimental and control groups, standardized achievement measures, and other means of ensuring the objectivity and reliability of the findings. The studies took place in urban, rural, and suburban schools all over the U.S. and in three foreign countries, and involved a wide range of subjects and grade levels.

Johnson and Johnson also have reported significant gains in student achievement as a result of cooperative learning. They have published 43 studies over the past 12 years. Their studies, using control groups, were carried out in primary through college-level classes in a variety of subject areas. They also have conducted surveys and laboratory studies and found gains in academic achievement for all age levels in a variety of subject areas.

Although more research has been done at the elementary level, Newmann and Thompson (1987) summarized research on the effects of cooperative learning at the secondary level. They identified 27 reports that met their methodological criteria for matching control and experimental (cooperative learning) groups. The 27 reports yielded 37 comparisons of control and experimental (cooperative learning) methods. Of these, 25 (68%) favored the experimental method for overall academic achievement at the .05 level of significance.

Newmann and Thompson go on to point out that cooperative learning approaches may be less acceptable to secondary students. Students at this age are less responsive to rewards and other forms of recognition. They may be under pressure to cover large amounts of material and therefore expect their teachers to give them a lot of information through lectures. Often their previous school experiences have taught them to value individual achievement and to be competitive. Given these constraints, teachers wanting to implement cooperative learning in secondary schools will need to spend time teaching cooperative skills and orienting students to the different classroom procedures that cooperative learning requires.

Intergroup Relations

Most studies of intergroup relations have used sociometric measures (Whom would you like to work with on a class project?), behavioral observations, or peer ratings. In general, research has found that students who work in a racially mixed group develop more friends outside of their own racial group. However, studies vary in their reporting of the length and intensity of these friendships. In cooperative learning groups, students from different racial backgrounds work together on a common goal. In the process they learn to appreciate and respect each other. Just as important is that working in a racially mixed group may reduce previously held negative attitudes. More research is needed in this area.

Providing for Mainstreamed Students

Ballard and his colleagues (1977) conducted some of the earliest field experiments to study acceptance of special needs students by regular students. They found that educable mentally retarded students in the experimental (mainstreamed) groups were better accepted by their classmates. Later studies have confirmed their findings. Studies also show that mainstreamed students have improved classroom behavior and greater self-confidence.

These studies have particular significance for cooperative learning, which provides a natural way to increase the interaction and friendships between regular students and special needs students. In fact, cooperative learning could be considered as an ideal way of implementing mainstreaming in a school.

Self-Esteem

The research shows that cooperative learning can have a positive effect on self-esteem. According to the ASCD Research Information Service (1981), "Cooperative learning methods are aimed at reducing student isolation and perceived hostile climates that exist in highly competitive classrooms and at increasing students' ability to inter-act and work with other students toward common goals." Eliminat-ing the highly competitive environment and replacing it with a supportive one gives students a feeling that they can achieve. When peers help each other learn, lower-ability students feel there is a chance to succeed. When they experience success, they feel confident about their academic abilities. When students use the Jigsaw model, each one is responsible for a specific body of information, which is indispensable for the success of the group. Therefore, each student feels important. The friendships that develop from working together on a task contribute to self-esteem. Finally, the satisfaction of com-pleting a project successfully and being recognized for it enhances self-esteem.

Summary

In the typical classroom, students meet their learning objectives individually or competitively. However, another option exists: organizing students in cooperative learning groups. Such groups provide the opportunity for positive independence among students who share the responsibility for learning and develop leadership and communication skills.

Research indicates that group goals and individual accountability are important conditions for cooperative learning. Further, cooperative learning leads to improved academic achievement and positive intergroup relations, provides for mainstreamed students, and enhances self-esteem.

Cooperative learning encourages greater acceptance of the differences among students. They learn by cooperating not competing. Student initiative is encouraged, self-esteem is enhanced. Students learn cooperative and communication skills that can transfer to other academic and social situations as well as to life in general.

References

Aronson, E., *The Jigsaw Classroom*. Beverly Hills, Calif.: Sage, 1978.

ASCD Research Information Service. "Highlights from Research on Cooperative Learning." *Educational Leadership* (May 1981): 659.

Ballard, M.; Corman, L.; Gottlieb, J.; and Kaufman, M. "Improving the Social Status of Mainstreamed Retarded Children." *Journal of Educational Psychology* 69 (1977): 605-11.

Bohlmeyer, E.M., and Burke, J.P. "Selecting Cooperative Learning Techniques: A Consultative Strategy Guide." *School Psychology Review* 16 (1978): 36-49.

Burns, M. "Groups of Four: Solving the Management Problems." *Learning* (September 1981): 46-51.

Deutsch, M. "An Experimental Study of the Effects of Cooperation and Competition upon Group Process." *Human Relations* 2 (1949): 199-232.

Johnson, D.W., and Johnson, R.T. "Toward a Cooperative Effort: A Response to Slavin." *Educational Leadership* (April 1989): 80-81.

Johnson, D.W., and Johnson, R.T. *Learning Together and Alone: Cooperation, Competition, and Individualistic Learning*. Englewood Cliffs, N.J.: Prentice-Hall, 1987.

Johnson, D.W., and Johnson, R.T. *Learning Together and Alone: Cooperation, Competition, and Individualization*. Englewood Cliffs, N.J.: Prentice-Hall, 1975.

Johnson, D.W.; Johnson, R.T.; Holubec, E.J.; and Roy, P. *Circles of Learning*. Fairfax, Va.: Association for Supervision and Curriculum Development, 1984.

Johnson, D.W.; Johnson, R.T.; and Maruyama, G. "Interdependence and Interpersonal Attraction Among Heterogeneous and Homogeneous Individuals: A Theoretical Formulation and a Meta-Analysis of the Research." *Review of Educational Research* 53 (1983): 5-54.

Kagan, S. *Cooperative Learning: Resources for Teachers.* Riverside, Calif.: University of California, 1985.

Kagan, S. "Co-Op Co-Op: A Flexible Cooperative Learning Technique." In *Learning to Cooperate, Cooperating to Learn*, edited by R. Slavin, S. Sharan, S. Kagan, R. Hertz-Lazarowitz, C. Webb, and R. Schmuck. New York: Plenum, 1985.

Newmann, F.M., and Thompson, J.A. "Effects of Cooperative Learning on Achievement in Secondary Schools: A Summary of Research." Paper from National Center on Effective Secondary Schools, University of Wisconsin, Madison, 1987.

Parker, R.E. "Small-Group Cooperative Learning: Improving Academic, Social Gains in the Classroom." *NASSP Bulletin* (March 1985): 48-57.

Sharan, S., and Hertz-Lazarowitz, R. "A Group-Investigation Method of Cooperative Learning in the Classroom." In *Cooperation in Education*, edited by S. Sharan, O. Hare, C. Webb, and P. Hertz-Lazarowitz. Provo, Utah: Brigham Young University Press, 1980.

Sharan, Y., and Sharan, S. "Group Investigation Expands Cooperative Learning." *Educational Leadership* 47 (December 1989/January 1990): 17-21.

Slavin, R.E. *Cooperative Learning Theory, Research and Practice*. Englewood Cliffs, N.J.: Prentice-Hall, 1990.

Slavin, R.E. "Research on Cooperative Learning: Consensus and Controversy." *Educational Leadership* 47 (December 1989/January 1990): 52-54.

Slavin, R.E. "The Cooperative Revolution in Education." *Education Digest* (September 1988): 22-24.

Slavin, R.E. *School and Classroom Organization*. Hillsdale, N.J.: Lawrence Erlbaum Associates, 1988.

Slavin, R.E. "Cooperative Learning and Individualized Instruction." *Arithmetic Teacher* (November 1987): 14-16.

Slavin, R.E. *Using Student Team Learning*. Baltimore: Johns Hopkins University Press, 1986.

Slavin, R.E. "An Introduction to Cooperative Learning Research." In *Learning to Cooperate, Cooperating to Learn*, edited by R. Slavin, S. Sharan, S. Kagan, R. Hertz-Lazarowitz, C. Webb, and R. Schmuck. New York: Plenum, 1985.

Slavin, R.E. "Synthesis of Research on Cooperative Learning." *Educational Leadership* (May 1981): 657.